Original title:
Fern's First Fragments

Copyright © 2025 Creative Arts Management OÜ
All rights reserved.

Author: Jaxon Kingsley
ISBN HARDBACK: 978-1-80567-026-1
ISBN PAPERBACK: 978-1-80567-106-0

Emerging from the Crust of Time

In the soil, a curious sprout,
Wonders what the world's about.
Poking questions through the muck,
"Do I need to dress or just get pluck?"

Rabbits giggle as they pass,
"Look at that, a flowered class!"
Frogs croak tunes of rhythm and rhyme,
While dirt stains slip, a punchline in time.

Nature's Palette of Possibilities

Colors splash like paint on a rock,
Sunflowers gossip, making them talk.
"Did you see the bee in that pink dye?"
"I wish he'd just learn to fly by!"

Doodles of clouds in the sky so bright,
Play tag with shadows, a comical sight.
Each hue a giggle, a jaunty cheer,
Nature blending laughs, far and near.

Echoing the Breath of Spring

Springtime squeaks like a rubber shoe,
Waking up the sleepy dew.
Squirrels start to dance and twirl,
"It's time to make our acorn whirl!"

Buds burst forth with a giggling sound,
Flowers compete to be the crown-bound.
"Who has the best color, can you guess?"
"Oh please, it's all about the mess!"

The Beauty in New Beginnings

A tiny seed starts a fresh debate,
"Am I a flower or a salad plate?"
Roots wiggle with a curious flair,
"Maybe I'll grow an audience there!"

Daisies offer a joyful jest,
"Let's see who can bloom the best!"
In this garden of chatter and cheer,
Every sprout giggles; spring has drawn near.

The Promise of Soft Sprouts

A tiny bud bursts forth with glee,
Whispering secrets of what might be.
The world looks on, quite unimpressed,
Yet the sprout reveals its hidden quest.

In soil it wiggles, roots all around,
A dance of life beneath the ground.
"Watch me grow!" it shouts, quite absurd,
While passing squirrels chuckle and curd.

In the Hands of Nature's Craft

Nature's fingers nudge and poke,
Crafting odd shapes, a charming joke.
An acorn dons a hat of grass,
While worms debate who'll be first to pass.

With a splat and a plop, the rain shimmies,
Turning puddles into leafy skimmies.
Grass blades wear sunglasses on sunny days,
Daring the world to join in their plays.

Celebrating the Fledgling Green

A tiny leaf waves to the bees,
Pondering life in a light summer breeze.
"Look at me!" it shrieks with flair,
While crickets play tunes with flair to spare.

Saplings wiggle, stomp and dance,
With roots so wobbly, they take a chance.
Each newly sprouted spore has a tale,
Of mischief and laughter on every trail.

Threads of Light and Life

Threads of sunlight weave through the trees,
Tickling leaves and teasing the breeze.
The grass giggles 'neath feet that stomp,
While butterflies dance and slightly romp.

A world of wonder, silly and bright,
Each sprout a comedian, ready to bite.
In this garden of smiles, laughter is free,
As flowers boast of their polka-dot spree.

In the Cradle of Spring

Bunnies bounce with joyful cheer,
And flowers giggle year by year.
Ladybugs wear spots so fine,
While robins sing of sunshine wine.

Clouds drift by in fluffy race,
While squirrels dance, they keep their pace.
The sun plays hide-and-seek with trees,
As laughter echoes on the breeze.

The Awakening Earth

Turtles wear their tiny hats,
As whispered jokes fly 'round like bats.
Bees buzz in a comic tune,
While daisies laugh beneath the moon.

Worms are wriggling, making plans,
In their little underground clans.
With every sprout, a giggle sings,
As nature teases with tiny wings.

Awash in Lush Reverie

Butterflies with painted wings,
Swirl and twirl, they share their flings.
The brook laughs as it skips along,
Singing silly, watery songs.

Frogs croak jokes in rhythmic time,
While crickets chirp in playful rhyme.
The grass sways like a dancer's floor,
Inviting everyone for more.

New Beginnings in Dewdrops

Morning dew on leaves so bright,
Like little jewels, what a sight!
Ants march on in silly rows,
Carrying crumbs as nature's prose.

Sunshine tickles every blade,
As nature's laughter won't degrade.
With every dawn, a brand new joke,
In the garden where dreams evoke.

Strokes of Sunlight

In the garden, shadows play,
Sunbeams dance, a bright bouquet.
Butterflies giggle, a feathered show,
Tickling flowers as they grow.

The ants march home with tiny snacks,
While snails chill out, riding on tracks.
A bumblebee hums a cheerful tune,
Sipping nectar, beneath the moon.

Laughter blooms in the morning dew,
Every leaf whispers secrets anew.
The sun stretches wide, yawns to the east,
As a silly squirrel hosts a feast.

With each glance, the world seems wild,
Like a jester in a garden styled.
Petals chuckle, roots rejoice,
Nature sings with a playful voice!

Illuminated by Nature's Touch

A wobbly worm with a fancy hat,
Swaying around, how about that?
Sunshine tickles the treetop high,
As the breeze helps the daisies sigh.

A cheeky robin steals the show,
Dancing on branches, stealing the flow.
The flowers clap, they can't sit still,
While buzzing bees take up the thrill.

Caterpillars munch on leafy greens,
Creating chaos in their dreams.
Each petal sways with laughter loud,
Nature's antics drawing a crowd.

Glowworms sparkle, dimples bright,
In the twilight, a funny sight.
Nature giggles, no need for a crutch,
Life is a laugh, illuminated by touch!

Emergence in the Quietude

In the stillness, whispers roam,
A hedgehog prances, finding home.
Mice wearing hats, oh what a sight,
Giggling softly under moonlight.

The pond splashes, frogs leap high,
Croaking jokes that make clouds sigh.
A chase begins, a race, not slow,
As the fish laugh, putting on a show.

Stars twinkle, winking in delight,
While crickets chirp, ready to unite.
The owl hoots jokes, wise and bold,
In nature's pause, fun unfolds.

Every shadow hides a grin,
As laughter spills from within.
Emergence here is truly bright,
In the quietude, joy takes flight!

Tender Roots

In the garden where whispers grow,
The plants giggle and put on a show.
Under the sun, they wiggle and sway,
Conspiring secrets in their leafy ballet.

A dandelion's wish flies with bliss,
While a potato dreams of a life full of risk.
With roots intertwined, they laugh and they tease,
Chasing each other on the warm summer breeze.

Rising Spirits

With morning dew, the fun begins,
As worms host a race on their tiny skins.
Birds chirp like they're passing a joke,
While squirrels play cards beneath the oak.

The sun stretches lazy, like a sleepy cat,
As bees buzz around in a furious spat.
Laughter erupts from the tulips so bright,
Each petal whispers tales of pure delight.

The Dance of Soft Shadows

In the twilight glow, shadows prance,
A ballet of giggles, they leap and dance.
The lamppost chuckles at the sight so grand,
While crickets play tunes in a one-limbed band.

A cat in the corner, plotting with glee,
Whispers, 'Watch close, for the show's just for me!'
As moonbeams twinkle, the shadows take flight,
Spinning and twisting into the soft night.

Embrace of the Unseen

Invisible friends play peek-a-boo,
Rustling leaves whisper, 'Guess who?'
A breeze carries laughter, soft and bright,
While ants parade 'neath the fading light.

With each footstep, secrets unfold,
Of muddy puddles and dreams bold.
They giggle and wiggle, a wild charade,
In this hush of twilight, where fantasies are made.

Lush Reveries

Bouncing blossoms hold a friendly chat,
While a gnome tells tales of an old, silly cat.
They ponder the art of the best shade,
In hopes that the sun gives a joyful parade.

A snail with a top hat glides with flair,
Chasing a shadow without a care.
Together they plot, with laughter combined,
To turn each moment into a find.

Sprinkles of Light

The fireflies gather for a shimmering spree,
Painting the night with giggles and glee.
A chorus of chuckles, twinkling and bright,
In a joyous festival, lost to the night.

Among the grass, secrets bloom and sprout,
Whispering laughter is what it's about.
With each little spark, they dance in delight,
Bringing magic and mischief, oh what a sight!

Dreams Woven in Tendrils

Laughter sprouts from tangled hair,
A leafy world where giggles flare.
With every twist and turn we sway,
In leafy dreams, we jump and play.

Tiny creatures dance with glee,
Wearing hats made of chamomile tea.
They whisper secrets, then take flight,
As we swing by, oh what a sight!

A giggling tree gives us a spin,
As squirrels join in, let the games begin!
With acorns bouncing, oh what a noise,
Nature's playground for girls and boys.

In this wild place, the sun peeks through,
Painting shadows of every hue.
We tumble and roll without a care,
Wrapped in joy, a perfect affair.

Adrift in a Sea of Leaves

Surrounded by leaves, I'm a lost boat,
Sailing on laughter in a tiny float.
Each gust of wind tells a funny tale,
As the trees sway, oh how we sail!

Leaves tickle noses, a playful tease,
As we chase each other, doing as we please.
The ground is a trampoline, soft and bright,
Bouncing through autumn with pure delight.

A crooked branch holds a sign that reads,
"Help! I've lost my favorite seeds!"
With giggles erupting, we gather near,
Making up stories with shouts of cheer.

Drifting along this leafy sea,
Each swish and rustle is pure glee.
In this green boat, we laugh and glide,
In nature's humor, we find our ride.

The Softening of Winter's Grip

Winter's chill is losing the race,
As laughter blooms in every space.
Frosty fingers start to fade,
Chasing warmth where kids have played.

Snowflakes giggle, throwing a ball,
While under them, we begin to sprawl.
The sun peeks out with a knowing grin,
Inviting us to dance and spin.

The icicles melt with a feeble clink,
As puddles form for a quick drink.
With splashes and squeals, we jump right in,
Splash fights and sneezes—let the fun begin!

Woolen hats toss away their frowns,
As the world shakes off its winter gowns.
In the merry thaw, we sing and play,
Welcoming spring on this joyful day.

Silence Between the Petals

In the garden blooms a silent jest,
Where flowers giggle, it's quite the quest.
Petals whisper amongst the bees,
Chasing each other in the warm breeze.

The tulips curtsy, the daisies cheer,
As butterflies twirl their dance so dear.
With every flutter, a chuckle springs,
Such joy the blooming season brings!

An ant on a mission, serious face,
But trips on dew, such a clumsy grace!
Laughter erupts from the softest rose,
In the sunny warmth, fun overflows.

In this garden, a symphony plays,
Of rustling leaves and sunny rays.
Between petals lies silence so sweet,
A perfect backdrop for laughter's beat.

In the Embrace of Untamed Flora

In a jungle of jolly green,
Laughed a vine with a wobbly sheen.
It tickled a tree with a giggle and sway,
And whispered jokes to the bugs at play.

A flower donned shoes made of fluff,
Said, "Dancing is easy, but I'm not that tough!"
The bees spun around in a dizzying whirl,
While sharing their secrets with a laughing pearl.

A leafy hat waved to passersby,
Inviting the sun for a warm, playful cry.
With petals for friends, they formed a parade,
And the shadows beneath swayed to joy unafraid.

As the bees buzzed tunes from a nearby hive,
The flora conspired to feel more alive.
In this garden of giggles, bewitching and grand,
The wild laughter echoed, a magical band.

A Symphony of Vibrant Greens

The trees conducted a rustling tune,
While bushes broke out in a chuckling croon.
A cactus danced awkwardly in a line,
Saying, "Coordination just isn't divine!"

Leaves tossed a party with snacks made of dew,
While the sunbeams painted a colorful view.
A clumsy snail slid by with a grin,
Claiming, "I brought my best friends from within!"

The petals of daisies clapped in delight,
As the wind played a melody, breezy and light.
"Let's twirl and whirl beneath the big sun!"
Cried the joyful greens, so happy to run.

In this symphony bright, every shade took a chance,
Finding rhythm and laughter, they formed quite a dance,
With a chorus of colors, they sang from afar,
Creating a laughter-filled world under the star.

The Art of Layered Shadows

In a garden of giggles, shadows took shape,
Playing tricks like mischievous tape.
One shadow pranced, stepping out of line,
Saying, "Dare to dance? It'll be just fine!"

Another whispered, "I can't take the heat,
Let's hide behind flowers and retreat, retreat!"
But the sun laughed loud, lighting the way,
As the shadows wobbled and started to sway.

A petal climbed high on the back of a breeze,
Flaunting its colors as it danced with ease.
"See, I'm the queen of this playful parade!"
Shouted the shadow, no longer afraid.

In the hilarity of light and dusk blend,
The giggles echoed, a cheerful trend.
With everything layered and comically bright,
The art of their laughter was sheer delight.

Shapes of Light and Leaf

In the antics of daylight, leaves turned to dance,
They flipped and they flopped in a happy romance.
A butterfly sighed, "Oh, look at that flair!"
While the shadows just grinned, pretending not to care.

Shapes played together in whimsical flight,
Doodles of laughter in soft, gleaming light.
The sun threw a party, and all were invited,
But the shadows, of course, were a bit undecided.

"Do we shadow today, or should we just glow?
Why not both?" said a whisper, "Let's put on a show!"
With giggles and jests, they painted the ground,
In a swirl of delight where happiness found.

Shapes of bright laughter and leaves in a spin,
Filled the air with a cheer, like a whimsical win.
In the playful ballet of bright, leafy beams,
Joy danced alongside as they spun their sweet dreams.

The Dawn of Delicate Life

In the garden, a sprout does tease,
A tiny leaf dances in the breeze.
Birds gossip over breakfast crumbs,
While ants march loudly, tapping their drums.

The sun peeks in, a cheeky grin,
Waking up bugs with a tickle and spin.
A ladybug flaunts her polka-dot show,
As shadows of daisies chase after the glow.

Threads of Nature's Innocence

A spider spins, with flair so fine,
Weaving webs like a crafty design.
Flies buzz in, unaware of their fate,
While crickets are laughing, they just can't wait.

A caterpillar munches without a care,
Dreaming of wings but not quite there.
Butterflies giggle as they float away,
Leaving the worm confused in dismay.

Echoes of an Unfolding Tale

A bloom pops up, with colors so bright,
Shouting, 'Look at me!' from morning till night.
Bees come buzzing, in a busy rhyme,
While frogs croak tunes, keeping lazy time.

A snail takes a stroll, but oh so slow,
Wonders aloud where the cool flowers grow.
A breeze whispers laughter, a playful tease,
As petals flutter down like confetti leaves.

Petals in the Breeze

Wind carries secrets in a wild ballet,
Tickling each blossom that sways in play.
Squirrels scamper, stealing the show,
While frolicsome puppies chase after a toe.

Dandelions scatter with a puff and cheer,
Wishing on wishes that fly, oh so near.
Ticklish grass tickles toes as you run,
In this dance of nature, oh, it's just too fun!

Lush Dreams Beneath the Surface

In the soil, giggles hide,
Worms in parties, side by side.
Roots are whispering all around,
Planting jokes beneath the ground.

Little seeds in cozy beds,
Dream of beans and slumbering spreads.
They tell tales of sprouting cheer,
While critters laugh and share a beer.

Tiny leaves with big ideas,
Trading dreams with tiny peers.
Who knew that growth could be so wacky?
In the garden, nothing's tacky!

So here we are, a leafy crew,
With sunbeams shining, we'll break through.
A vibrant song beneath the sod,
Nature's humor, on the pod!

The Magic of Unseen Growth

Underneath the world so vast,
Roots are dancing, oh, so fast!
They twirl and leap without a sound,
In secret skies beneath the ground.

A sprout says with a cheeky grin,
"Can't wait to show my leafy skin!"
Hidden magic, growing tall,
Nature's laughter, here for all.

Wiggly worms will cheer and shout,
As to the sun, we all scout out.
So many dreams lie just below,
With every drop of rain, they grow.

Who knew roots could crack such jokes?
Why do they never fear the hoax?
With a wiggle and a surprise swoop,
We burst alive—what a funny troop!

Beneath Skyward Stems

Beneath the stems that climb so high,
Laughter bubbles, oh my, oh my!
Fronds are tickling as they rise,
With tiny giggles, they surprise.

The ground's a stage for sprouty plays,
For worms in tuxes, they dance all day.
Frogs jump in with a mighty leap,
In this garden, quit your sleep!

Little sprouts whisper and scheme,
Dreaming big is their main theme.
"Ow, my roots!" one softly quips,
Nudging friends with wobbly tips.

As petals boast of hues so grand,
The secret chuckles, unplanned.
Riding breezes, we are free,
In this green world—what joy to see!

Chasing the Sunlit Path

On sunny paths, where shadows play,
Little shoots come out to sway.
With a jiggle and a hop,
"Here comes the sun!" they chant and stop.

Five-leaf clover, what a find!
"Join our dance; don't fall behind!"
Nature's disco, twirl and spin,
With roots so strong, let fun begin!

Prancing buds in morning light,
Invite the world, all in sight.
They spread their leaves and share a joke,
In every breeze, the laughter spoke.

So step with glee on this bright trail,
Join the fun, your worries pale.
Life is thriving, green and shy,
In laughter's arms, we all comply!

Treading on Fresh Soil

In the garden, mud-stained shoes,
Wiggly worms in a silly snooze.
Trowels dance like they've got a say,
Making plants giggle, come what may.

Muddy paws and laughter sprout,
Jumping puddles, there's no doubt.
A sunflower wearing shades of fun,
Can't stop laughing under the sun!

With hiccups loud from the frogs so bright,
They croak out jokes in the moonlight.
Garden gnomes with silly grins,
Plotting mischief as the day begins.

So let's laugh as we dig and toil,
Creating joy in this fresh soil.

A Mosaic of Leaves and Dreams

Crinkly leaves, a patchwork scene,
Squirrels chuckle, their coats all green.
A dance of colors, a vibrant cheer,
They giggle at visions that magically appear.

A leaf fell down, so delicate,
Wobbled and rolled—oh, what a fate!
It joined up with a bit of fluff,
And suddenly life got a bit more tough!

Rain drops drumming, a silly tune,
Charming critters under the moon.
They whisper secrets, oh so grand,
Of adventures held in leaf-filled hands.

In dreams we twirl, a leafy parade,
Making funny faces as they invade!

The Heartbeat of the Forest Floor

Listen close, can you hear the beat?
Dancing mushrooms with wiggly feet.
The forest floor's a stage so grand,
Where acorns cheer, and critters band.

Twirling ferns with a prancing glee,
Chasing shadows, wild and free.
A hedgehog in a tiny hat,
Wondering where his friends are at!

Raccoons with masks, gearing for play,
Stealing snacks in a sneaky way.
Nutty giggles echo through trees,
The heartbeat of fun carried in the breeze.

With every step, laughter spreads wide,
Nature's giggle cannot be denied!

Enchanted Beginnings in Green

Bright buds sprout in endless cheer,
Starting their journey, drawing near.
A ladybug winks, decked in spots,
While the sun winks too, tying knots!

Tiny sprouts peek, just for a glance,
Joining leaves in a whimsical dance.
A caterpillar spins tales with flair,
Dreaming of wings and scenic air.

Twirling petals, oh, what fun!
Colorful jokes from everyone.
In this garden, magic's in sight,
Creating laughter from morning till night!

So here's to beginnings, fresh and bright,
A world of giggles, pure delight.

The Language of Young Shoots

Little sprouts with silly hats,
Whisper words of pollen chats.
They giggle as they stretch so wide,
Telling tales of wormy slides.

Wiggly roots play hide and seek,
In the soil, they dance and peek.
Sprigs of laughter fill the air,
As they wiggle without a care.

Tiny leaves in colors bright,
Debating who's the cutest sight.
With each breeze, they sway and bend,
Making mischief with a friend.

Gentle Hues of Growth

In shades of green, they tease and play,
Dressed in outfits for the day.
With straws of sunlight, sipping cheer,
They share secrets no one hears.

Dandelion puffs float by,
Telling jokes as they fly high.
Wink at clouds, and giggle too,
As they toss their seeds like confetti, woo-hoo!

Caterpillars wearing coats,
Writing songs on water boats.
Every twig a stage, a scene,
In their world of leafy green.

A Dance Among the Shadows

Underneath the leafy quilt,
Dancing critters, none are built.
They twirl and swirl, all around,
In the shade where laughs abound.

Mushrooms giggle on their toes,
While shadows play with funny clothes.
Socks of dirt and hats of mist,
Join the fun; you can't resist!

The moon peeks in with a wink,
To hear the jokes, they start to think.
Cicadas hum and crickets sway,
As the night paints funny play.

Secrets Beneath Soft Canopies

Beneath layers of leafy death,
Secrets hide with whispered breath.
Furry critters plotting schemes,
While beneath, the soil's dreams.

A log rolls in to join the fun,
Bringing jokes from the sun.
Mushroom friends, all dressed in white,
Add a twist to the starry night.

Funky roots in a tangled mess,
Discussing who wears the best dress.
In this quiet, playful brawl,
Nature laughs as a chorus calls.

A Symphony of Sable Laces

In a garden where laughter blooms,
A squirrel danced among the brooms.
With laces tied too tight and strange,
He somersaulted, quite deranged.

A bird on a swing made of thread,
Sang tunes that spun inside my head.
While bees in hats buzzed round and round,
Chasing their tails without a sound.

Potatoes played their violin,
As carrots joined—with a chubby grin.
They jived atop the leafy stage,
While wise old toads turned the page.

So come, dear friend, let's twist and shout,
In this garden where fun's the route.
With every giggle, joy's embraced,
In this symphony, laughter's traced.

Chronicles of the Gentle Frond

A frond once fancied itself a hat,
On a passing cat—it tiptoed, flat.
With giggles shared in leafy notes,
They danced like oddball, merry goats.

The daisies whispered secrets sweet,
To snails that shuffled on tiny feet.
While ladybugs donned capes of red,
Claiming to rule from the flowerbed.

The butterflies held a tea so grand,
With cups made from the finest sand.
And ants, with ties, took notes so fast,
Of tales that never seemed to last.

So roam with me through fronds so bold,
Where laughter blooms and stories unfold.
Each leaf a giggle, every petal—glee,
In this gentle realm of hilarity.

Beneath the Canopy of Hope

Beneath the leaves, the fun commenced,
A frog in shorts sat, quite condensed.
He croaked a tune, sang off-key frights,
While crickets chimed in, buzzing delights.

A turtle dressed in polka dots,
Raced with a hare, and tied the knots.
With cheers from bugs, it seemed so wild,
Oh what a sight—a slower child!

They spun beneath the starry twink,
Sharing their thoughts o'er cups of drink.
From acorns served on silver sprouts,
To dreams that danced and jumped about.

So let's dive deep into that play,
Where laughter guides us through the day.
In nature's show, the joy is bright,
A canopy of endless light.

Awakening in Shades of Emerald

In emerald realms where laughter grows,
The grass wore pants, as everyone knows.
With colors bright and quirks abuzz,
The flowers laughed, saying, "Just because!"

A caterpillar spun a yarn,
About a worm who broke his barn.
With jokes so bad, they made bugs cry,
Yet still, they roared with laughter high.

A windmill turned, now twisting hight,
With chimney pots that wobbled bright.
And trees recited riddles tight,
As shadows danced in gleeful flight.

So join the chorus, sing along,
In nature's grip, where all belong.
With sprigs of humor blooming wide,
Awake to joy, let's take a ride!

Whispers of New Beginnings

In a pot, a sprout did peek,
With leaves so small, it gave a squeak.
"Why am I stuck?" it seemed to say,
"Get me out, let me play all day!"

The sun above, a blazing grin,
"Oh dear sprout, let the fun begin!"
A dance of shadows, a twist of light,
Comical moments all day and night.

Raindrops giggle on leafy heads,
As worms below spin goofy threads.
Each new bud, a prankster's delight,
With every inch, they spark a fight.

In this patch of chaos, joy takes root,
With snickers and chuckles, all out astute.
So lean in close, and hear them cheer,
For sprouting dreams are finally here!

The Unfolding Leaf

A leaf unfurls with a little flop,
"Look at me!" it gives a hop.
But wait, what's that? A tiny bug,
A ticklish friend, oh give a hug!

The laughter spreads like morning dew,
As ants parade, a marching crew.
"You're upside down!" the leaf will tease,
With wiggles and jiggles, oh what a breeze!

Each tiny breeze brings tales anew,
Of daring jumps and silly do's.
With every twirl, the laughter grows,
As plants share jokes, nobody knows.

So toast to leaves and roots that play,
In their green world, come what may.
With silly giggles, they'll always weave,
A tapestry of joy we cannot believe!

In the Shadow of Green

In the shade, a secret crew,
Tiny plants with mischief to pursue.
"Shh!" they whisper, eyes all aglow,
As the sun sets, it's time for the show!

A dandelion wearing a crown,
"I'm the king!" it shouts, "Bow down!"
But a buttercup rolls in, quite proud,
"Not so fast!" it laughs out loud!

Together they play hide and seek,
A leap here, a shimmy, midweek peak.
The shadows shake and twist around,
As these green sprites dance, so profound!

With sighs of joy, the moon peeks in,
"Are you still at it?" it grins with a spin.
In the shadow of green, laughter reigns,
With silly whispers, joy never wanes!

Echoes of Tender Growth

In a corner of the garden space,
New sprouts giggle as they find their place.
"Look at us!" they cheer, all bright,
With mischief brewing, pure delight.

A row of peas, all in a line,
"We're more than just green, we can shine!"
They wiggle and jostle, full of glee,
Throwing a party, just wait and see!

Carrots in their underground show,
"So much fun, but no one will know!"
They wiggle deep, sharing a laugh,
While radishes plan their silly half!

Each echo sings of laughter and bloom,
In every nook, joy does consume.
Tender growth speaks with a jesting tone,
In the garden of giggles, no one feels alone!

Sprouting from Forgotten Earth

In a garden where weeds do roam,
A sprout danced, calling dirt its home.
It wiggles, it jiggles, oh what a sight,
Claiming to be a flower, just out of spite.

The raindrops giggle, they splash and tease,
As worms do the tango, with effortless ease.
Each day is a party, they're having a ball,
While the old, wise rocks just watch from their stall.

A leaf in a breeze sings a silly tune,
While ants march in line, all wearing a spoon.
They're cooking up mischief, right under the sun,
It seems that the garden is never outdone.

So if you feel small, or lost in your way,
Remember the laughter that sprouted one day.
From forgotten earth, where oddities play,
Life's a chuckle, come join the fray!

Shadows Play in Morning Glow

Morning light peeks, with shadows in tow,
A squirrel in shades puts on quite a show.
He flips and he flops, a critter with flair,
While daisies pretend that they just don't care.

Underneath trees, a picnic unfolds,
With ants plotting schemes, oh so bold!
A sandwich goes missing, who could it be?
The culprit looks round, then grins with glee.

A dandelion dreams of being a star,
But all that it gets is a breeze from afar.
It fluffs up its hair, and oh, what a mess,
As petals provide a hat, no less!

So raise up your cup, enjoy the fun,
In shadows that dance, where the wild things run.
The morning's alive with laughter and cheer,
Just follow the giggles, you'll find them near!

The Tenderness of Leafy Lullabies

Beneath leafy roofs where the crickets sing,
A lullaby curls like the comfort of spring.
Frogs croak their verses, a rhythm so sweet,
While the stars twinkle down, keeping time to the beat.

A caterpillar dreams of a great butterfly,
But mostly it munches on lettuce nearby.
With crumbs on its face, it sighs with a grin,
"Who needs to fly when I can eat tin?"

Branches embrace in a warm, leafy hug,
While the moon dips low, like a cozy, soft rug.
The fireflies dance in a shimmering row,
Their flickers like secrets, all aglow.

So rise with the sun, greet the laughter in line,
For in nature's song, we find joy divine.
With lullabies soft and the night's tender pleas,
Laughs branch like trees, carried on the breeze!

Musings in the Canopy

In the canopy high, where the ideas collide,
A parrot debates with a witty old guide.
"Should I mimic the crow or stick with my song?
A peachy decision can't be wrong for long!"

A squirrel takes notes, furiously scribbling,
While a wise old owl just sits, giggling.
"Be yourself!" it hoots, "Not so hard, just try!
The best copycat's one who can't tell a lie!"

Little acorns gather to share thoughts so bright,
Spinning tales under the pale moonlight.
"I'll grow into a tree, just you wait and see!"
While the mushrooms just ponder, "Will it be me?"

So if you're stuck up in life's leafy maze,
Just climb a bit higher and bask in the rays.
In musing together, we learn to be free,
With laughter in branches, oh, what a spree!

Whispers from the Foliage

In the garden where giggles grow,
Leaves rustle with tales of woe.
A squirrel sneezes, a bird takes flight,
While worms take bets on the next moonlight.

Sunbeams play tag on the grass below,
A snail sprints past, just moving slow.
Every leaf holds a secret grin,
Trying hard not to let laughter win.

The daisies gossip in colors bright,
Sharing stories by morning light.
With each plop of raindrop's sound,
Petals bounce, swaying round and round.

And if you listen, there's a song,
Of frolicking critters where they belong.
Mossy benches where fairies meet,
Tickling toes in this leafy retreat.

A Tapestry of Untold Journeys

In the tangle of roots, a tale unwinds,
Of wayward creatures and silly finds.
A chipmunk's map leads to the fridge,
While crickets plan a midnight bridge.

The ladybug leaps with tiny flair,
Her dance moves get caught in the air.
And if a beetle joins in the fun,
You bet the flowers will start to run.

Moles dig deep, but miss all the laughs,
Digging for treasure in their own little paths.
While fireflies flicker like stars at dusk,
Sharing their light in a world of husk.

Each vine is woven with joy and jest,
A tapestry bold—nature's best.
Where every creature's a part of the show,
And laughter blooms wherever you go.

The Quiet Chorus of Life

A hush falls gently on the leaf's crest,
As a critter tunes up for the best.
The breeze hums softly with a light twist,
While worms wiggle to join in the list.

Beetles beat drums on a raindrop stage,
A grasshopper croaks like a bard of the age.
Toadstools tap dance in their own high heels,
And ladybugs giggle with all their feels.

In shadows, the spiders weave threads of glee,
Creating art no one else can see.
The ants clap in rhythm, marching in line,
Celebrating a party that's simply divine.

So gather around, join the quiet cheer,
In the secret world, there's nothing to fear.
Each bug and leaf in melodic play,
Can turn the ordinary into a ballet.

Beneath the Soil's Secrets

Underneath, where the critters scheme,
Worms are plotting the ultimate dream.
A rave for roots is set to unfold,
With each little burrow, their stories told.

The gophers giggle at the crops above,
While moles throw parties with tunnel love.
Cabbages dance in line like pros,
Beets whisper secrets nobody knows.

The earth's a canvas, and we're all the brush,
Painting the ground in a vibrant hush.
As tiny feet shuffle in playful delight,
A festival brews under soft moonlight.

So next time you walk on the grassy plain,
Remember the laughter beneath the grain.
For every step you take toward the sky,
There's a whole underground party waiting nearby.

Gathering of Young Leaves

Tiny buds are peeking out,
Chasing away the winter's pout.
With a giggle and a jig,
They dance like leaves on a twig.

Shiny greens in morning light,
Wiggling roots, what a sight!
Silly sprouts play hide and seek,
In the garden's lively creek.

In a breeze, they sway and play,
Whispers of a sunny day.
Little arms reaching wide,
Ready for a leafy ride!

Frogs croak out their merry tunes,
As the seedlings belt their swoons.
Who knew greens could be this fun?
A leafy band has just begun!

Realms of Seedlings and Sunlight

Sprouts are plotting in a row,
Underneath a sunlit glow.
With a wink and a big grin,
They stretch out to soak it in.

Dirt is flying, seeds take flight,
Bouncing like they're filled with light.
Each little leaf a grand charade,
Growing up, an escapade!

Butterflies flit here and there,
Tickling leaves without a care.
Every giggle, loud and clear,
In this realm, there's naught to fear.

Sing a song, my green friends bold,
In your world, tales unfold.
Life's a giggle, bright and fast,
In the garden, joy's amassed!

A New Chapter Written in Green

A page turned with leafy cheer,
Humming tunes for all to hear.
Sprouts recite their playful rhymes,
In the glow of sunny climes.

Laughter bursts from every leaf,
Each one a playful little thief.
Stealing sunlight, warmth, and glee,
Planting hints of mystery.

Twirling about in playful glee,
Writing stories, just like me.
Tiny whispers in the breeze,
Invite the world and all it sees.

With every wiggle, tiny tease,
Each little root starts to seize.
A brand new chapter filled with zest,
In nature's heartbeat, we are blessed!

Tendrils of Hope Unfurl

Outreach fingers stretch and sway,
In a whimsical display.
Tiny tendrils twist in flight,
Reaching for the sky so bright.

A tickle from a morning breeze,
Gives them joy and makes them please.
Growing wild, they'll steal the show,
A comedy of green aglow!

Whispers rustle, secrets shared,
Every sprout has someone cared.
With a laugh, they spread around,
Nature's magic can be found.

Tendrils giggle, roots turn red,
As they play tag, no time for dread.
In this world, all is just right,
As the greens prepare for night!

Secrets Held in Papery Folds

In a crumpled pouch, secrets lie,
Whispers of leaves that flutter and sigh.
A paper trail of giggles and glee,
Scattered stories as bright as can be.

Beneath the sun, a dance of delight,
Silly shapes play, what a curious sight!
A fold here, a crease there, tales untold,
Chasing rainbows that spark and unfold.

What's hidden between these fragile sheets?
A treasure of laughs, oh what funny feats!
Smiling stems and a chuckling bud,
In this playful garden, who needs a flood?

So come take a peek, and don't be shy,
Secrets are laughing, just give them a try.
In papery folds where giggles reside,
Join in the fun, come take a ride!

A Journey Through Verdant Hues

Through shades of green, we boldly roam,
In turtlenecks made of lichen foam.
Bouncing on vines like a bouncing bean,
Nature's playground—oh what a scene!

A whisper of mint in the breezy air,
I tripped on grass—now isn't that rare?
Frogs wear tuxedos, ready to perform,
While squirrels debate the merits of charm.

With each step, a new hue will greet,
And leaves shimmy down, oh what a treat!
Dandelions giggle, their fluff in a twist,
Join in the chaos, you simply can't resist!

So gallivant forth, through color and cheer,
In this happy garden, it's all crystal clear.
A journey that's silly, with nature in flow,
Laughing with plants as they steal the show!

The Art of Nature's Revival

From the ashes, a sprout takes a chance,
In the rhythm of growth, it starts to dance.
Little green fingers, waving to the sky,
"Hey, look at me!" they shout, oh my!

Wiggling worms below, laughing so loud,
As daisies bloom, they're hell-bent on proud.
A toss of the seed, and then what a sight,
Nature's own sketch, painted in bright light.

The sun sprays laughter on thirsty lips,
While critters around share their little quips.
With petals like giggles, they flutter and sway,
In this art of revival, silliness plays.

So paint your world in colors so loud,
In every sprout's joy, simply feel proud.
Nature's own canvas, filled with delight,
Laugh with the blossoms, it's pure, it's right!

Gentle Hands and Gifted Seeds

With careful hands, seeds gently drop,
Into the earth, they bubble and pop.
What fun to see, as sprigs yawning rise,
In a race to the sun, beneath bluest skies.

Dancing in pairs, the seedlings grow,
With whispers of dreams in the wind that blow.
They wiggle and giggle, spreading out wide,
As nature's own laughter takes us for a ride.

Tiny toes peek through the soft, brown crust,
"Look at us!" they brag, "We've grown, we must!"
From gifted hands full of playful cheer,
These sprightly newcomers know no fear.

So plant those seeds, let the fun begin,
In a garden of giggles, you'll surely win.
With gentle hands and smiles that please,
Watch nature unfold, oh do as you please!

Brush of Nature's Tender Hand

A dandelion danced in the breeze,
With dreams of becoming a lion with ease.
But it sneezed and it laughed, oh what a scene,
As it floated away, a fluffy little queen.

The sun winked down with a cheeky grin,
Tickling the petals, inviting them in.
A bee buzzed a tune that was far from sweet,
As it tripped on a daisy, losing its beat.

Worms in the dirt held a comedy club,
Sharing their tales of the famous mud scrub.
With jokes about rain and a puddle or two,
They rolled on the ground, just to amuse you.

The wind played a game, a tickle and tease,
Whispering secrets through the rustling leaves.
Nature's a jokester, and oh, how it thrives,
In this world where the laughter forever survives.

Greenheart's Gentle Murmurs

In the depths of the woods, the critters conspire,
A squirrel climbed high just to find some desire.
But a nut went astray, oh what a delight,
As it rolled down the hill, causing a fright.

A turtle named Ted had big plans to race,
But tripped on a root and fell flat on his face.
His friends all chuckled, 'Come try it again!'
But Ted just smiled and said, 'Not my zen!'

A frog croaked a joke that went over their heads,
About slimy old socks and wormy old beds.
The laughter erupted, so loud in the glade,
Even the owl woke with a scruffy charade.

Mushrooms giggled as they swayed on their stalks,
Sharing tall tales of who could outfox.
Nature's a comedy, full of surprise,
With each chuckle echoing under blue skies.

Tapestry of Unraveled Green

There once was a leaf that fell from a tree,
It told all the others, 'Come fly just like me!'
But a windstorm was brewing, and oh, what a fuss,
As they tumbled and spun, like a wild circus bus.

The grass had a party, the kind that you crave,
With worms as the dancers and ants as the brave.
They shuffled and jived, in a messy old line,
Stepping on daisies, thinking they were divine.

A caterpillar grumbled, 'I need a new look!'
But his friends all agreed, 'You're the best in this book!'
So they dressed him in leaves, with a hat made of moss,
And he posed like a guru, so proud, he'd emboss.

The breeze hummed a tune nobody could find,
Refusing to settle, winding and twined.
In nature's art gallery, laughter rings clear,
A tapestry woven where humor is near.

Fragments of Nature's Whisper

A flower was chatting with a rock on the ground,
Saying, 'I bloom pretty, but you, you astound!'
The rock chuckled back, 'Well, life's quite a trip,
But the best part is snacks, I'll share if you whip!'

The clouds overheard, in their fluffy white coats,
And decided to play, tossing raindrops like boats.
Nature erupted in giggles, oh what a sight,
As the puddles turned giggly, but soaked everyone right.

A centipede offered to host a big race,
But tripped on his legs, oh the silly disgrace.
His friends all erupted in a fit of delight,
As he rolled in the grass, what a comical sight!

With whispers and laughter, nature unfolds,
In the forest of wonders, a story retold.
The fragments of joy dance along the path,
In a world where the funny stirs nature's own wrath.

The Veil of Dew-Kissed Dreams

A morning mist starts to gather,
As leaves play hide and seek with laughter.
The sun peeks through with a grin,
Whispering tales of where it's been.

Tiny bugs dance with delight,
While mushrooms giggle, dressed in white.
A frog hops by, wearing a crown,
Claiming the throne of the teeming town.

In shadows deep, the critters hide,
While squirrels in suits take a joyride.
Each dewdrop sparkles like a prank,
As nature's children fill their tank.

A gust of wind shakes off the surprise,
As pollen floats, tickling our eyes.
The world awakes and starts to sing,
To celebrate the joy of spring.

Morsels of Soft Growth

In the soil, stories take their shape,
Wiggly worms in a giggly scrape.
Little sprouts whisper, "We're on our way!",
With dreams of sunshine brightening the day.

Tiny ants march in a straight line,
Carrying breadcrumbs like they're fine wine.
Each slip and trip brings hearty peals,
As they swap stories about their meals.

Patches of green throw a cheeky dance,
While daisies tease bees for a glance.
With roots entwined, they plot the scene,
Creating chaos, fresh and serene.

The garden laughs, its heart so wide,
As critters join in, with joy, with pride.
Every leaf a comedian in play,
In this gamboling green cabaret.

A Journey Beneath Spiraling Stems

Down below where the secrets creep,
Mushrooms gossip while the shadows leap.
Twisting vines share tales of old,
Of rambunctious buds that dare be bold.

Rabbits perform in a leafy stage,
While beetles argue, both wise and sage.
A beetroot dances with goofy flair,
Causing the carrots to puff and stare.

Twisted roots sing a playful tune,
While fireflies flash under the moon.
Each moment here feels like a game,
Where the flowers laugh and share their fame.

In tunnels deep, the party's wild,
With nature's laughter, carefree and styled.
A journey here is full of cheer,
Where every corner bubbles with glee.

The Voice of the Quiet Grove

In the grove where whispers dwell,
Trees exchange secrets, none can tell.
A breeze carries a chuckle or two,
As branches sway for a playful view.

Mossy carpets cushion their feet,
While mushrooms gossip and dance on repeat.
The shadows tease with flickering light,
Inviting all creatures to join the night.

Each rustle prompts a round of applause,
As crickets chirp with charming cause.
Leaves giggle softly, brushing the ground,
While laughter echoes all around.

The quiet grove sings soft and low,
Yet fumbles on punchlines, just for the show.
In such sweet solace, all find a place,
Sharing their joy with a smile on each face.

Unraveled Dreams in Dew

In the morning light, I tripped on a root,
A dancing beetle laughed, in a tiny suit.
Confetti of petals fell from the trees,
While squirrels debated the best type of cheese.

Rabbits played poker, with acorns for chips,
And mushrooms were gossiping, sharing their tips.
The wind whispered secrets that only it knows,
As caterpillars strutted in brand new clothes.

Laughter erupted from a chubby old snail,
Who wore on his shell a bright, polka-dot veil.
The world woke up giggling, no frowns to be seen,
Each dew drop a jewel, each blade like a queen.

So if you find joy in the odd and the small,
Just take a deep breath and embrace it all.
For here, in this garden of whimsical cheer,
Life's silly fragments are perfectly clear.

Ferns at Dawn's Embrace

A frog croaks a tune, but it's slightly off-key,
As fireflies blink lights, like a disco marquee.
The sun yawns awake, with a stretch and a grin,
While the crickets are lost in a twilight gin spin.

A snail zooms on, leaving trails of pure slime,
Beneath him, a ladybug dances a mime.
The blossoms erupt in a colorful spree,
As shadows stretch long, sipping nectar like tea.

The grass tickles toes in a ticklish way,
As ants tell a tale of their wild, crazy day.
With a flick of the tail, a cat sneaks on by,
Though all of the birds just hoot, "Oh my, oh my!"

Dawn spins its magic in a laughter-filled breeze,
Unfolding adventures 'neath arching green trees.
In this blossoming world, every giggle's a prize,
As life bounces along with a wink in its eyes.

Nature's Silent Rebirth

With the hush of the night, the woodpecker snores,
A raccoon in pajamas just opens its doors.
The flowers swap stories in whispers so bright,
As shadows dance lightly, stealing moments of light.

A tiny chihuahua thinks it's a fierce beast,
Chasing down shadows, like a cat at a feast.
The trees shake their branches with laughter and cheer,
While ladybugs roll in a flower-shaped leer.

Old owls tell tales of the wild, wacky nights,
Where each tiny critter had fanciful flights.
Beneath the blue moon, the world starts to sway,
As each blade and petal holds dances at bay.

In this silence of life, with critters so spry,
Nature giggles out loud, painted deep in the sky.
Every heartbeat's a joke, every sigh's a delight,
As the morning creeps in, to conclude this silly night.

The Secrets of Sprouting Life

In the garden of giggles where daisies confide,
A worm in a monocle takes a grand ride.
He waves to a bumblebee, buzzing so loud,
Whose dance moves are surely for a vibrant crowd.

The soil burps softly under the new sun,
As little green shoots shout, "Let's have some fun!"
With a wink from the daisies, the petunias all sway,
While tulips throw confetti to brighten the day.

A curious crow with a snazzy black hat,
Perches near blooms, giving compliments flat.
The daisies all blush, turning pink with delight,
As the ferns chuckle softly in the shimmering light.

Each sprout tells a story, a jest or a pun,
In this rhythmic dance where the day's just begun.
Unraveled in laughter, the whole garden hums,
As life's little secrets burst into soft drums.

Hidden Pathways in the Wild

Beneath the brush, a secret trail,
A squirrel dons a tiny mail.
With acorns packed, he winks with glee,
On a quest for nuts, just wait and see.

A rabbit hops with stiff-legged grace,
Chasing shadows in a silly race.
While flowers giggle, clump and sway,
They know the jest of a sunny day.

An owl hoots down from his lofty post,
He'd rather laugh than be a ghost.
With wise old eyes and feathers fanned,
He's plotting pranks on the bunny band.

Each creature shares a playful jest,
In these wild paths, they feel their best.
Adventure waits with every turn,
In leafy lanes, we laugh and learn.

Echoing Life in Verdure

A leaf fell down with a gentle thud,
It plopped right in a puddle of mud.
A frog jumped high, trying to land,
But slipped and slid, oh, wasn't it grand!

The trees all swayed and told a joke,
Whispers floated like a funny cloak.
A breezy breeze chimed in with cheer,
'Life's a laugh, let's give a cheer!'

Bumblebees buzz with a silly tune,
Dancing in circles, under the moon.
They bumble and tumble, they laugh, they play,
Creating joy in the light of day.

So let us join this vibrant spree,
In every leaf, a joke to see.
With each small laugh, the world expands,
In the green, we'll all make plans.

Whispers of Young Leaves

Young leaves rustle, secrets share,
They tickle branches high in the air.
A windy giggle runs through the woods,
As nature chuckles, feeling good.

A butterfly flits, a painted prank,
Dancing through blooms on the riverbank.
With wings so light, it steals the scene,
Wearing a crown of dandelion green.

A beetle marches in a fancy hat,
Strutting along where the vines are at.
He tips his brim, a patron of flair,
Even the ants stop and stare.

Echoes of laughter in soft sunlight,
In this green world, everything's bright.
With every whisper and every tease,
The young leaves giggle in the breeze.

Unraveling Green Dreams

In the meadow, dreams float and twist,
A ladybug claims she can't resist.
With polka dots and winks so sly,
She tells the story of the sky.

A patch of clovers holds a ball,
Where grasshoppers gather, oh so tall!
Dancing madly, they leap and spring,
A revelry fit for a tiny king.

The sunbeam jester slides down slow,
Spreading warmth in a vibrant flow.
A swing of shadows, giggles abound,
In nature's laugh, joy is found.

So let's unfold these little dreams,
In tangled green where laughter beams.
With whimsy sprouting from every seam,
We'll sow our lives with happy themes.

www.ingramcontent.com/pod-product-compliance
Lightning Source LLC
Chambersburg PA
CBHW071833160426
43209CB00003B/281